Compliments of

The Haverford Trust Company
——*Investment Management*——

Three Radnor Corporate Center, Radnor, PA
610.995.8700   888.995.1979

PHILADELPHIA

A PHOTOGRAPHIC PORTRAIT

PHOTOGRAPHY BY
RICH DUNOFF

TEXT BY
PHIL WAGNER

First published in the United States
of America by:

Twin Lights Publishers, Inc.
10 Hale Street
Rockport, Massachusetts 01966
Telephone: (978) 546-7398
http://www.twinlightspub.com

ISBN 1-885435-51-7

10 9 8 7 6 5 4 3 2 1

Photography by:
Rich Dunoff
(610) 449-9979
www.phillyphoto.com

Text by:
Phil Wagner
(610) 688-2692
wagassoc@snip.net

Book design by:
SYP Design & Production, Inc.
www.sypdesign.com

Printed in China

Philadelphia is the shape of…well, who knows what? This city of proud neighborhoods—some 105-plus by last count—oddly configured as it is, sits hard against the Delaware River. Jammed into the southeastern-most corner of Pennsylvania, it looks across the Ben Franklin Bridge at southern New Jersey, from which a handsome slice of its daily workforce, avid sports fans and visitors come. Meanwhile, another river, the lesser Schuylkill, snakes through the city and under Interstate 95, augmenting the Delaware just above a smartly refurbished Philadelphia International Airport.

Maybe its imprecise fit is what makes America's fifth largest city the haven, both historic and hip, that it certifiably is. Just maybe the fact that their city has a Greater Northeast (as it's affectionately known), a northwest, a center city and a west-southwest—but no true east section—is what makes "Fluffadelphians" the passionate breed that they so birthrightly and forthrightly are.

Two hours south of New York, a little more drive time north of D.C., sits William Penn's crowning achievement in the Commonwealth bearing his name. This "greene Countrie Towne" that Penn is thought to have originally traded honorably for with indigenous Lenni Lenape Indians, whom his sons would later deceive, works. Fascinates. And, as the service hub that it is, impacts the global economy daily in such industries as finance, insurance, real estate, communications, management investment, electronics, pharmaceutical, and medical/health care. Notwithstanding W.C. Fields' faint praise, its myriad offerings today broadly transcend the qualities of religious freedom and economic opportunity that so attracted Penn.

From Fishtown, Roxborough or Gray's Ferry to Bridesburg, Southwark or Chestnut Hill, the 1.5 million who call Philadelphia home, care—monstrously—about their mayor, their Mummers, their Eagles (a.k.a. Iggles), their heritage…and their eats. From cheesesteaks to Tastycakes to scrapple to Philadelphia (not made here!) Cream Cheese. For them, life radiates out from City Hall, where Broad (actually, 14th) and Market Streets intersect. They take Penn's gridded street design, and America's "most historic square mile" nestled in its midst, absolutely for granted. To them, this tourist mecca is home.

Beyond the maze of iconoclastic neighborhoods, nearly 9,000 acres of Fairmount Park creates a gateway to "the burbs," where another four million Greater Philadelphians enjoy the most reasonably priced housing market from Boston to D.C. plus superb schools. Many live along the (old Pennsylvania Railroad's) Main Line, running west to Downingtown or so. Out here *The Philadelphia Story* exploded on screen. And, a spit away, the King of Prussia Mall grew to second largest in the land.

Much that's shaped, and shapes, America has happened in this cradle of liberty where a cracked bell draws a curious world; and where national treasures like Washington's headquarters at Valley Forge National Park (20 miles to the west) beckon unspoiled. Since only a weighty tome could suggest it all, this photographic portrait focuses on Philadelphia proper, known as "Athens of the Americas" in the 18th century, and as City of Brotherly Love still.

Final thought. "As the city that gave us the Declaration of Independence and the Twist, William Penn's principles of peace and purity and the soft pretzel, Philadelphia can be both significant and lighthearted," a Fodor's 2002 travel guide understates. Surely this vibrant place can be those two things…and everything else you care to make it!

Western Exposure

Running parallel with its namesake river, the Schuylkill (cynics say, *Surekill!*) Expressway is the main commuter route from Valley Forge and the city's western suburbs into Center City. About this 25-mile road originally envisioned as a parkway, its design engineer advised, "If you don't like it, don't drive it." Quite a few don't, and don't.

(above and left)

Philadelphia City Hall

Designed by John McArthur, Jr. and topped by William Penn, the massive 642-room building is America's largest city hall. Elaborate detail work integrating architecture and sculpture festoons the exterior of this colossus more than three decades in the making.

(above and opposite)

At Broad and Market

The tallest masonry-bearing building in the world—at 547' the tallest building in Philadelphia until 1987—City Hall boasts more than 250 pieces of sculpture outside and inside, most attributable to Alexander Milne Calder. His 27-ton, 37' bronze William Penn on top is the largest single piece of sculpture gracing any building in the world.

(above)

Franklin over Vine

This quirky negative-space rendition of Benjamin Franklin and lightning bolt sits on the 17th Street bridge over the Vine Street Expressway.

(opposite)

From a Floral Perspective

City Hall, projected to be the tallest building in the world, had by the time it opened at the turn of the last century, lost out to the Eiffel Tower and the Washington Monument. Love Park is in the foreground.

Game Time

Outside the city's Municipal Services Building playful sculpture dominates, much of it having to do with household game pieces. That's a Parcheesi piece on the left, dominoes on the right (an old Philadelphia variation of which is called Sniff).

(right and opposite)

(above)

The Big Bambino

Francis Lazzaro Rizzo, who jumped from being police commissioner to the city's two-term Democratic mayor throughout the 1970s, died in '91 while contemplating a fifth run. To him, "A conservative is a liberal who was mugged the night before."

(left)

Love Sculpture

Robert Indiana's brightly painted aluminum icon graces Kennedy Plaza in what's known as Love Park. After it was moved to New York, local citizen F. Eugene Dixon bought and returned the sculpture to Philadelphia.

(opposite)

Masonic Temple

This National Historic Landmark with its seven lodge halls houses both the Grand Lodge of Free and Accepted Masons, and the Masonic Library and Museum, of Pennsylvania.

(above, left and opposite)

Philadelphia Museum of Art

Cultural jewel of the city, this mythic structure of Minnesota dolomite designed by Julian Francis Abele sits on 10 acres and boasts 200 galleries. That's Chief Justice John Marshall holding court at right.

(above)

Art Overview

An aerial shot makes explicit the sprawling museum's location on "Faire Mount" (thus, Fairmount Park), sitting as it does at the western end of the Benjamin Franklin Parkway, close by and above the Schuylkill River.

(left)

Rocky's Footprints

Rocky Balboa, a.k.a. Philadelphia native son Sly Stallone, is immortalized here at the Museum of Art, yet his bronze statue from this spot now adorns the city's sports complex to the south. Though there are actually 99 steps, Rocky bounded up only 72 on film.

(above and right)

Art Everywhere

In the Museum's north pediment, Carl Paul Jennewein's polychrome terra cotta figures of Zeus and gang celebrate sacred and profane love, while outside the west entrance, Louise Nevelson's corten steel *Atmosphere & Environment XII* beckons.

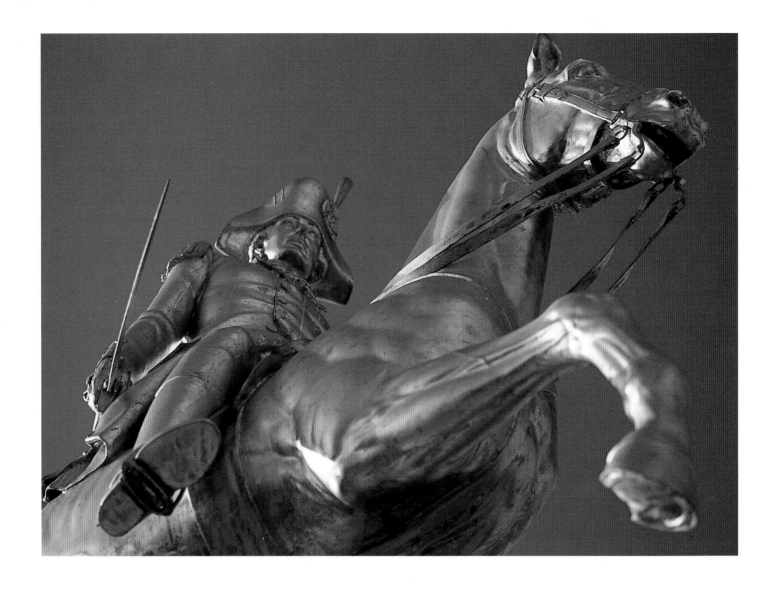

"Mad Anthony"

Stationed near the Art Museum, that's
General "Mad Anthony" (or Ant'ny in South
Philadelphia-ese) Wayne, after whom the
town of Wayne in the city's Main Line
suburbs is named.

(above and right)

River Runs Through It

The Schuylkill River enters Center City here from the west, along Boathouse Row, as a single sculler heads out of town. At bottom are two of 32 bridges over the meandering river.

(above and opposite)

Crew is King

Philadelphia, long known as a bastion of rowing worldwide, hosts (among many others) the Dad Vail Regatta, largest collegiate event in the nation, and the Stotesbury Cup for competitors from more than 100 high schools nationwide each May. Boathouse Row is an aggregate of Gothic Revival, Italianate and Victorian Gothic buildings.

(above, right and opposite)

Mixed Architectures

Frederick Graff's Fairmount Water Works, on five acres just below and behind the Art Museum, comprise a National Historic, Civil and Mechanical Landmark. Housing an acquarium for decades into the 1950s, they ensured a potable water supply to the city throughout the 1800s. Federal, Tuscan, Gothic, Greek and Roman styles blend.

(above)

Joan of Arc

Emmanuel Frémiet's stately gilded bronze of French heroine Jeanne d' Arc, commands the start of Kelly Drive (formerly, East River Drive) out along the Schuylkill River.

(opposite)

Cathedral of Saints Peter and Paul

This basilica of the archdiocese of Philadelphia, contrasting architecturally as it does with its commercial neighbors, is spiritual home base for the metropolitan area's 1.5 million Roman Catholics. Its Italian Renaissance style copper dome was completed in 1864.

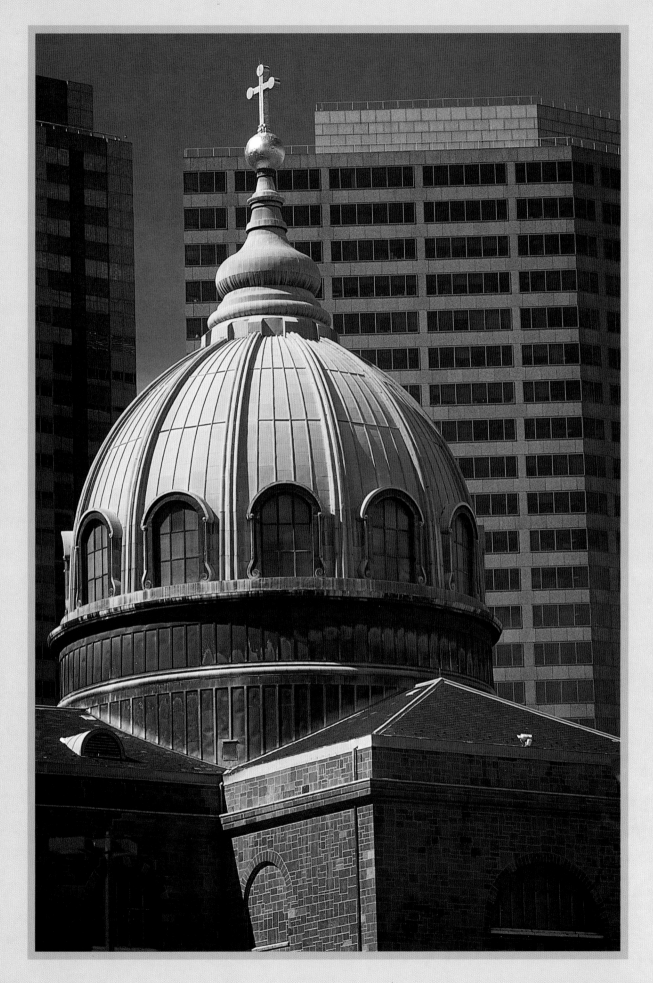

Washington on Franklin

Rudolph Siemering gets credit for this 1897 bronze rendition of Gen. George Washington, the latter facing down the Ben Franklin Parkway towards City Hall.

Swann Memorial Fountain

In this 1924 masterpiece by Alexander Stirling Calder at Logan Circle, bronze Indian figures represent the Delaware and Schuylkill Rivers plus the Wissahickon Creek, Philadelphia's three major waterways. Back in 1979, some 150,000 people saw Pope John II celebrate mass from a platform built over the fountain.

(above, left and opposite)

Academy of Natural Sciences

Founded in 1812 by the earliest paleontologists on this continent, this is a grand place to pet a tarantula, check out *T. Rex* or compare architecture. Known for its museum-education-research mission, the building houses over 17 million specimens. Audubon bird specimens, Lewis and Clark plant specimens and dinosaurs are on display alongside the oldest mollusk, fish and plant collections in the hemisphere.

(above and opposite)

The Franklin Institute

One square block of stimulation, imagination and interactivity on the Ben Franklin Parkway. This science museum is where people, especially young ones, come to see the 350-ton moving locomotive, stargaze in the Fels Planetarium or gasp in the Tuttleman IMAX® Theatre. Its mission: to inspire an understanding of and passion for science and technology learning. And to honor Ben Franklin eternally. That's him on the left, at 30 tons or so of marble, masterpiece of American James Earle Fraser also of "buffalo nickel fame."

Free Library of Philadelphia

Every bit the "fabulous freebie" it's often called, this public library system with its Greek Revival main branch at 19th and the Parkway offers almost 50 branches throughout the city.

(above)

Rodin Museum

Want to see the work of Auguste Rodin but you can't get to France? Well, this is the world's next best repository. First, of course, is *The Thinker*, symbolizing the universal artist and creative force. You'll pass though Rodin's 21' high *Gates of Hell* here, meet his famous sitter Balzac, and view Edward Steichen's photographic commentary.

(right)

The Great Doctor

Together with *The Great Mother*, the last works of Nazi Germany refugee Waldemar Raemisch in 1955, these two bronzes grace the outside of the Youth Study Center, facing the Ben Franklin Parkway.

Unmistakable Finial

The distinguishing shape on top marks Commerce Square by Pei Cobb Freed & Partners at 21st & Market Streets.

Breaking the Barrier

One Liberty Place, 947'-plus (spire included), became the tallest building in Philadelphia in 1987, when developer G. Willard Rouse boldly trumped an age-old gentleman's agreement that no building would surpass City Hall (today #7, at just 547'). Beside it is the Mellon Bank building.

Urban Geometry

As in all great American cities, skyscrapers and their lesser neighbors form striking architectural juxtapositions.

Can You See Me Now?

The Verizon Telephone Tower, née Bell Atlantic Tower by Kling-Lindquist Partnership, is an Arch Street standard.

(left)

Centre Square Plaza

Claes Oldenburg's whimsical 1976 corten steel *Clothespin* rises out of the depths as you exit the subway.

(right)

Cityscape Reflections

Photogenic buildings like Independence Blue Cross can become fuzzy, geometric abstractions through a Philadelphia filter.

(opposite)

Who's Going Higher?

One and Two Liberty Place by architect Helmut Jahn rule the roost in Philadelphia for now, but there's a new proposal afoot to build a 962' One Pennsylvania Plaza.

Philadelphia Skyline

Among the city's tallest buildings are (from left) Independence Blue Cross, Mellon Bank, One and Two Liberty Place.

Liberty Place

Aptly named in this city so identified with American liberty, One Liberty Place (middle) inspired a populace who, though emotionally bound by tradition, knew that onward was upward.

(above)

Ben Franklin Bridge

Connecting Philadelphia's waterfront with that of Camden, New Jersey, it's brightly blue by day, and brightly lit by night. A one-third-mile span made this the world's longest suspension bridge at its 1926 opening. Perched 150 feet above the Delaware River, it relies on 256 vertical cables.

(opposite)

30th Street Station

When you arrive by train in Philadelphia, you pass through this grand, vast building which many recognize from film classics such as *Witness* and *Blow Out*. Walker Hancock's pencil-thin bronze memorializes the Pennsylvania Railroad's WWII fallen.

(above)

Kimmel Center

The Kimmel Center for the Performing Arts, the latest star added to Philadelphia's Avenue of the Arts district, boasts 2,500-seat, cello-shaped Verizon Hall for the acclaimed Philadelphia Orchestra. Many companies perform in Rafael Vinoly's creation.

(left)

Union League

One of America's most historic and prestigious private clubs, this 3,000-member Grande Dame of South Broad Street claims leaders in many and diverse fields. Non-partisan, it was founded in 1862 expressly to support the policies of President Abraham Lincoln.

(above and right)

Bank Then, Hotel Now

Today's Ritz Carlton Hotel, formerly Girard Bank/Mellon Bank, was McKim Mead & White Architects' great Beaux Arts signature in Philadelphia. Offering 331 of the city's 10,000-plus hotel rooms, it's known for its elegance and marbled rotunda reproduction of the Pantheon in Rome.

Rittenhouse Square

One of five squares in the city representing a piece of what was once Penn's Woods, this residential haven was renamed (from Southwest Square) for astronomer David Rittenhouse in 1825, becoming the fashionable address for the Victorian aristocracy. More a neighborhood park than any other square today, the 6-acre passive use park was the only one of the five not used primarily as a burial ground. The Evelyn Taylor Price Memorial Sundial at left is by Philadelphian Beatrice Fenton.

(right and opposite)

Walnut Street

The Rittenhouse Plaza, one of Philadelphia's great Art Deco buildings, sits at 19th and Walnut Streets. To its far right on the north side of Rittenhouse Square is the Rittenhouse Club, once one of Philadelphia's storied men's clubs. Walnut Street is synonymous with elegant shopping.

(above, left and opposite)

The Pennsylvania Convention Center

Philadelphia welcomed conventioneers anew when it unveiled this magnificent venue in 1993. The Center's Grand Hall is the old Reading Terminal's restored 4-story Victorian train shed (broadest single-span shed in the world when built). Here's the Terminal's Italian Renaissance headhouse from different perspectives. Premier among thousands of events held here is the Philadelphia Flower Show each March, largest indoor horticultural event in the world.

(above)

Still Splendid

In Philadelphia, retrofitting and restoring means keeping all detail possible intact, such as this at the Pennsylvania Convention Center.

(left)

Oriental Welcome

Gotta have one... A Chinatown, that is, and Philadelphia emphatically does, north of Market Street. This 40' Friendship Gate, the largest such beyond China, announces *Philadelphia Chinatown* over 10th Street at Arch.

(above)

Outdoor Public Art

In Philadelphia, it's everywhere, by the city's 1%-of-construction decree. Ned Smyth's *World Park: Orders and Perspectives* outside the Marriott Downtown is rich in symbolism and reference to Greek, Egyptian and Byzantine architecture.

(right)

Market for the Ages

Behind the Convention Center remains the legendary Reading Terminal Market where Philadelphian, Pennsylvania Dutch and many other food specialties abound.

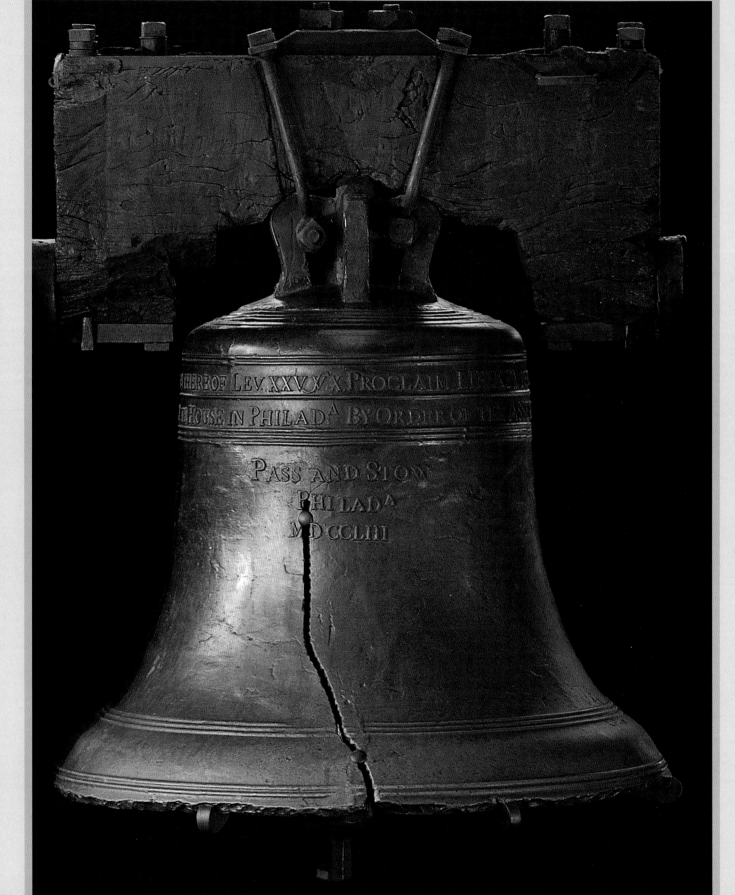

(above)

In the Gloaming

With the Art Museum at his back, America's first president (atop the monument bearing his name at Eakins Oval) surveys the 250'-wide Ben Franklin Parkway. Oft regarded as the nation's Champs Elysées, this roadway, designed by two Frenchmen, hosts more museums than any boulevard in the world.

(opposite)

Bell of All Bells

Known to all Americans, indeed symbol of freedom and liberty worldwide, this 2,080 pound monster of copper, tin and other metals newly resides in Liberty Bell Center at 6th and Market Streets, where it draws a million visitors annually. Embossed on it are the words *Proclaim Liberty throughout all the Land unto all the inhabitants thereof* (Leviticus 25:10).

(left, right and opposite)

"America's Most Historic Square Mile"

Independence Hall, commanding
Independence National Historic Park, was
originally known as the State House. The
Declaration of Independence and the
Constitution were signed here, the
Constitutional Convention was held here
and the Second Continental Congress met
here. That's Commodore John Barry out
front. Construction was completed in 1756.

(above and left)

Society Hill

Down near the Delaware, Society Hill offers upscale living and dazzling views of both the past and the river. That's the Todd House, with one of Philadelphia's signature sightseeing carriages, at 4th and Walnut. Dolly Payne Todd lived here, later to become Dolly Madison.

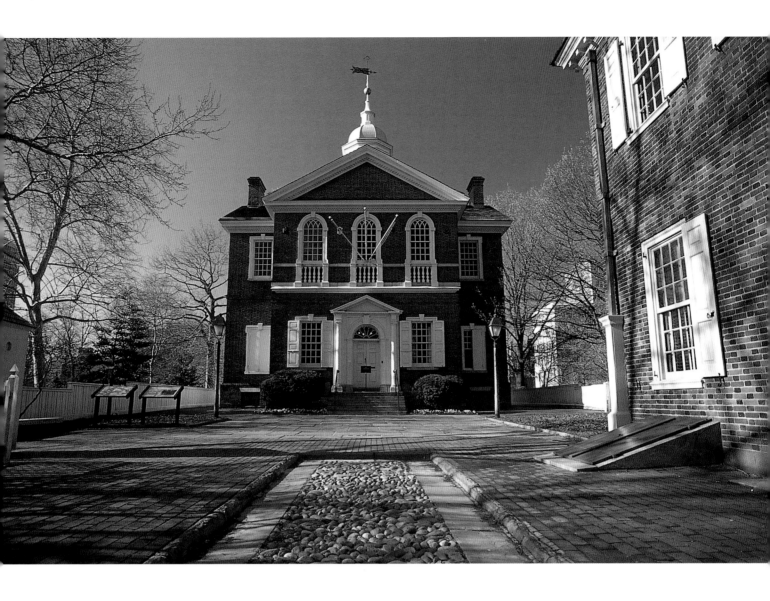

Carpenters' Hall

Here on Chestnut Street amidst Independence National Historical Park is where the First Continental Congress met in 1774.

SECOND BANK OF THE UNITED STATES

Independence National Historical Park

"The portico of the glorious edifice . . . always repays me for coming to Philadelphia."

Philip Hone, 1839

Here stands the Second Bank of the United States. Established in 1816 to hold government deposits and regulate currency, it dominated American finance for more than a decade.

The temple-like bank had both priests and heretics. Bank President Nicholas Biddle preached the value of the bank, while U.S. President Andrew Jackson decried it as a "hydra of corruption." The "temple" was looted of its treasure when Jackson vetoed the recharter of the bank, distributing government deposits to smaller banks.

Now, long after the passions of finance and philosophy have subsided, we recognize the architecture — not the institution — as the real treasure of the Bank. Designed by William Strickland, it has been called the finest example of Greek Revival architecture in the United States.

Andrew Jackson, President of the United States

Nicholas Biddle, President of the Second Bank

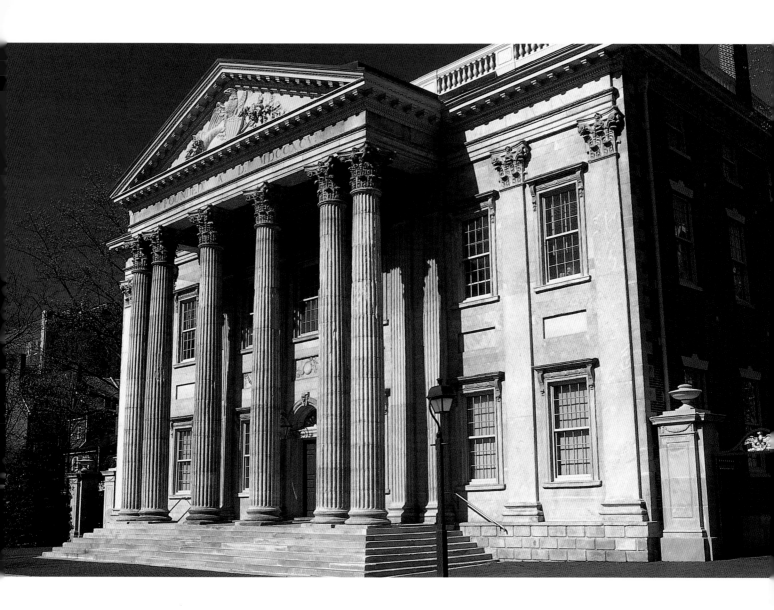

(above)

First Bank of the United States

Federal architecture at its best, America's oldest bank building housed the U.S. government's bank for more than a dozen years to 1811. Later, it was the private bank of Philadelphia financier Stephen Girard who bankrolled the War of 1812.

(opposite)

Second Bank of the United States

A sterling example of Greek Revival architecture on Chestnut Street, it houses a *who's who* portrait gallery of late 1700s luminaries, American and foreign.

(above)

Pennsylvania Hospital

Founded by Ben Franklin and Dr. Thomas
Bond in 1751, America's oldest hospital at
8th and Spruce Streets houses the first sur-
gical amphitheatre in the land. Outside,
John Bacon's 1774 lead rendition of William
Penn probably influenced Calder's Penn
atop City Hall.

(opposite)

Elfreth's Alley

Way back, much of Colonial Philadelphia
looked this way. Dating to 1702, this is the
oldest continuously occupied residential
street in the city (and nation), which publicly
showcases itself each June and December.

(left and right)

Federal Reserve Bank

No commercial bank, but rather a bank for financial institutions from the tri-state area under the auspices of the Federal Reserve System. Covering a block, its atrium features Alexander Calder's *White Castle* mobile, largest in the world, spinning slowly over a new *Money in Motion* exhibit. That's $100 million (shredded though) filling the tower.

(above and right)

Bourse Building

Once a commodities exchange in 1895, this remarkably restored building in the historic district beckons today with all manner of shopping and eating.

(above)

Merchants' Exchange

Closed to the public, this William Strickland Greek Revival edifice built on Dock Street in 1832 was Philadelphia's commercial hub for a half century, both stock exchange and trading post.

(opposite)

Was the Flag Sewn Here?

Betsy Ross may have lived here and may have made the Stars and Stripes here. Or may not. At any rate, this 8-room house on Arch Street (ca. 1760) epitomizes Colonial Philadelphia. For trivia, we do know that Ross, a good Quaker, outlasted three husbands.

Where Chiefs Lie

St. Peter's Episcopal Church at 3rd and Pine in Society Hill is a handsome church in continuous use since its inaugural September 1761 service. Seven Native American chiefs, who died of smallpox on a visit, are buried with Revolutionary war hero John Hazlewood, painter Charles Wilson Peale and important others. The Robert Smith-designed brick Palladian style building boasts a William Strickland steeple.

(left)

A Recognizable Look

Philadelphia's *Society* Hill neighborhood is full of Colonial-style and Federal-style brick rowhouses. It's where to live today just as it was in the 1700s. The area can thank the Free Society of Traders who followed William Penn here for its name.

(right)

Simple Meeting House

The Arch Street Meeting House dates to the earliest 1800s when the Philadelphia Yearly Meeting of the Society of Friends, i.e. Quakers, began convening here. The largest Friends meeting house in the world, it is a place of simplicity and quietude.

Tomb of the Unknown Soldier

This memorial to George Washington and the Revolutionary soldiers/sailors buried here highlights Washington Square, highbrow neighborhood as well as commercial publishing center. Its stone inscription reads: *Freedom is a light for which many men have died in darkness.*

Fort by the Airport

Sitting on the Delaware River which it was built to defend, just a spit from the city's international airport, is an austere Fort Mifflin, today a National Historic Landmark. Begun by the British, it was completed in 1776 by Revolutionary troops who, though vastly outnumbered during a 6-week battle against British foes a year later, ensured Washington's safe flight to Valley Forge.

(above and left)

Curtis Center Grandeur

This staggering 15' X 50' opalescent glass mosaic mural—*The Dream Garden*, derived from a Maxfield Parrish painting—more than commands the Curtis Center's lobby near Independence Hall. Installed by Tiffany in 1916, the mural features 260 distinct colors in a sea of hand-fired glass (some 100,000 pieces) and gold leaf. There's plenty of marble and granite in evidence, too.

(opposite)

Graff House

Here at 7th and Market Streets is where none other than Thomas Jefferson lived in 1776 while attending the Second Continental Congress and, most importantly, while drafting the Declaration of Independence.

(above)

From *A*(nt) to *Z*(ipperhead)

A contest in 1980 to name this punk rock clothing store on trendy South Street produced an easy winner: Zipperhead!

(opposite)

No Facelift Here

So often in Philadelphia, it's the outside that counts. This façade of an earlier department store fixture, Lit Brothers on Market Street East, now hosts an office complex with shopping gallery.

(above and opposite)

Gloria Dei / "Old Swedes' Church"

If you think Penn got here early, well, Swedes settled the area even sooner. This church in Southwark, plus an American-Swedish Historical Museum down near the sports complex, are most of what remains as proof.

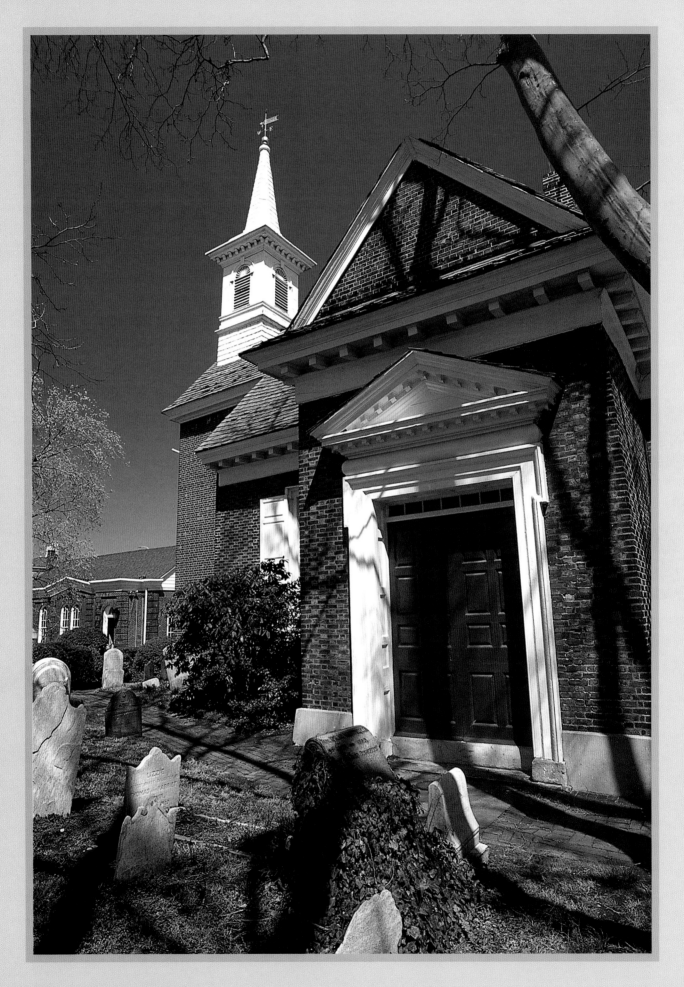

(above)

He Lives On, Evermore

The Edgar Allen Poe National Historic Site marks the only one of Mr. (*Quoth the Raven, Nevermore*) Poe's residences in the city spared the wrecking ball. He wrote such classics as *The Telltale Heart* whilst here for but one (1843–44) of his brief 40 years.

(opposite)

German Society of Pennsylvania

Back in 1683, thirteen German families founded America's first German settlement in, appropriately, Germantown to the northwest. Later this Society began in one of Spring Garden Street's stately buildings in 1764, making it the oldest such in the nation. The Joseph Horner Memorial Library is within.

National Constitution Center

The one and only museum in America dedicated to revealing and interpreting the U.S. Constitution to inquisitive visitors opened on Philadelphia's Independence Mall July 4, 2003. Interactive multi-media exhibits make the educational focus here both easy and fun.

World's Largest Mint

Got the 1776-1976 Bicentennial coin in your safe deposit box? Made in Phildelphia. Or a pocket full of quarters for the parking meter? Ditto. The U.S. Mint on Arch Street, king of America's four mints, can make 13.5 billion coins a year. To see 80,000 of its copper pennies in action, check out the Ben Franklin bust a block away.

(above, left and opposite)

Acclaimed Flower Capital

Philadelphia and environs are beyond rich in horticultural and floral beauty. From scenes like these in Independence Hall National Park to suburban arboretums, parks and gardens of all sorts, the area is renowned. And let's not forget the Philadelphia Flower Show each March, the nation's largest indoor spectacle.

(above, right and opposite)

Less is More

On Chestnut Street between 3rd and 4th is Franklin Court, Robert Venturi's steel outline of Ben Franklin's home and print shop, with post office and underground museum. This site amply attests to the ubiquitous Renaissance-Philadelphian's boundless genius.

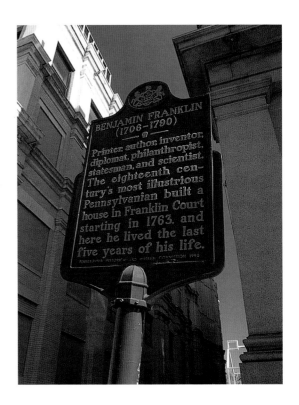

Penn's Landing Armada

On the Delaware River waterfront, two notable mainstays are the USS *Becuna*, a 328' "guppy class" sub whose 88-man crew ranged the South Pacific on WWII search-and-destroy missions, and the cruiser USS *Olympia*, Commodore George Dewey's flagship (and lone survivor from the Spanish-American War) when he kicked off the Battle of Manila with his immortal *"You may fire when ready, Gridley"* order.

Penn Landed Here

For all-around recreation, from outdoor to restaurants and nightclubs, Penn's Landing and its view across the Delaware can't be beat. Festivals, concerts and celebratory events of all kinds take place here throughout the clement months.

Sunrise on the Delaware

Ships tall and short punctuate the sun's daily
routine along Penn's Landing. When finished
here, one can ferry across the river to take
in Camden's waterfront attractions, like the
USS *New Jersey* and the New Jersey State
Acquarium.

Spanning Franklin

Of all things named in his honor throughout
Philadelphia, the Ben Franklin Bridge is certainly the most massive memorial. At its
base entering the city off a 1750' main span,
the icing on the cake is Isamu Noguchi's
101' high *Bolt of Lightning* memorial sculpture extending up from key on kite.

(above)

Stroller Motion

The South Street pedestrian walkway (one of three) high over Route 95 leads to the *Moshulu* and *Spirit of Philadelphia* docked on the Delaware, among other attractions. On it is William King's *The Stroll.*

(opposite)

Tall Ships Welcome

Whether back in the 1976 Bicentennial or in more recent times, when tall ships come to Philadelphia they make their way along the Delaware to the very shore where Penn landed in 1682.

(above, left and opposite)

Tugs, Talls and All

Small boats, big boats, short ships, tall ships—all at one point or another churn up the Delaware to visit Penn's Landing, and a small number stay on as permanent attractions. The Independence Seaport Museum is one of the many offerings along Christopher Columbus Boulevard, and near it is the ferry dock for crossing the river to Camden.

(above)

Woodford

Ben Franklin often visited this late-Georgian mansion designated a National Historic Landmark in 1980. It's completely furnished as an 18th-century Philadelphia home.

(left)

Ormiston

The red brick, late Georgian-style building belonging to this door-knocker dates to 1798, focusing on the Delaware Valley's British heritage.

(opposite)

Laurel Hill

Rawles-built in 1763-64, this mansion earned its name from sitting on a laurel-covered hillside overlooking the Schuylkill River. The Pennsylvania legislature confiscated it during the Revolution due to its owners' Loyalist sympathies.

21-Stone Salute

This Victorian Gothic, Ohio House, uses stone from 21 Ohio quarries, each identified via engraving. Constructed for the Centennial here as Ohio's exhibition building, and restored in the mid-1970s, only it and Memorial Hall still stand from that exposition.

(above)

Behind Woodford

Away from the stately main building at Woodford in east Fairmount Park, this out-building in a more rural scene complements the grounds.

(right)

Sweetbriar

Unchanged since 1797, this 3-story Federal mansion called Sweetbriar was built with floor-to-ceiling parlor windows overlooking the Schuylkill.

Glendinning Rock Garden

Fairmount Park is a maze of open space and tree stands, highlighted by stately mansions, recreational facilities and gorgeous gardens, like this one out Kelly Drive past Boathouse Row.

Pleasant Mount Pleasant

Just as the Chippendale influence had crested in America, this symmetrical Georgian country villa materialized at the hands of a Scottish sea captain. Benedict Arnold, it is said, bought it as a wedding gift for his smitten bride, but the matter of his treason conviction precluded their occupancy.

(above and opposite)

Embracing the Schuylkill

Two of a million scenes throughout
Fairmount Park, these cherry blossom trees
and rock garden steps provide sanctuary
within a busy city. Some two million trees,
with 100 miles of trails, elegant historic
homes, tons of sculpture and even cultural
institutions dot Philadelphia's recreational
paradise, which both Schuylkill River and
city itself divide. The world's largest land-
scaped urban park—from 8,500 to 8,900
acres depending on your source—this
playground is for all ages.

(above)

From Nagoya with Love

Reproduction of a 17th century scholar's house (or *shoin*), this teahouse and garden built in Japan ended up in Fairmount Park in 1958. Officially called Pine Breeze Villa (*Shofuso*) but known just as the Japanese House, it sits by the Horticultural Center.

(opposite)

Fairmount Park Horticultural Center

Statues may not outnumber trees, but they abound. This one is by Beatrice Fenton.

Horsing Around The Park

Reminiscent of Franklin Court's skeletal
structure, this 1993 stainless steel horse
sculpture called *Gambol II* by Robert David
Lasus romps behind the Japanese House.

(above and right)

Remember Memorial Hall

When Philadelphia geared up for the nation's 1876 Centennial Exposition, Hermann J. Schwarzmann's beaux arts stone and glass edifice made a nice art museum (predating that now on the Parkway). Atop the cupola stands Columbia, *"the hand presenting no sword, but the peaceful bays; the bowed head of salutation and welcome"* to the 10 million who came to celebrate. Her companions represent Industry (left) and Commerce (right).

(above, left and opposite)

The Philadelphia Zoo

Bearded pigs and Matschie's tree kangaroos—come see them and more than 2,000 other animals from six continents at America's first zoo, opened in 1874. An Amphibian and Reptile House, Primate Reserve, Carnivore Kingdom, Bird House, African Plains, Rare Animal Conservation Center, plus Treehouse and Children's Zoo, draw all ages through all seasons. Its 42-acre Victorian Garden showcases the naturalistic exhibits for which, among other things, this zoo is known worldwide.

(above and left)

An Academic Village

The University of Pennsylvania is just across the South Street Bridge from Center City. Its campus and presence have grown well beyond the original Quadrangle with undergraduate dorms (*above*) and Franklin Field (*left*), where the Penn Quakers play and the Philadelphia Eagles did into the 1960s. Penn, first in America to be designated a "university" and one of the Ivies, abuts neighboring Drexel in University City.

Benched Ben

Ben Franklin founded the University of Pennsylvania in 1740. This Seward Johnson sculpture on Locust Walk fools more than a few while reminding all of the close association.

(above and opposite)

Furness at Penn

Architecture commands attention throughout the Penn campus, and no name (but
Louis Kahn's) is as important as that of Frank
Furness. This Philadelphian's influence
abounds, and his Fisher Fine Arts Library
demonstrates why. As innovative a library
building as existed in America at its 1890
completion, it first served as Penn's main
library. Replete with gargoyles, its exterior
raised eyebrows at the time.

(above and left)

One Day, 156 Miles

The Wachovia USPRO Championship Bicycle Race held every June is, at age 20 in 2004, the longest-running and richest single-day cycling race in America. Its 156-mile course includes 10 trips up Manayunk's killer 17% grade landmark, The Wall, along which many of the half million faithful watch blood, sweat and gears triumph over matter.

Any Day, Any Mileage

For a gentler pace, bike along the river (Schuylkill) drives, an 8.4 mile loop from the Art Museum out to East Falls and back. Philly's one of America's top 10 bike-friendly cities, says *Bicycling Magazine*, with 150 miles already in place of a 300-mile net-work-to-be. Every May, there's even a Bike to Work Day.

Neighborhood Maze

Port Richmond is a working class North Philly neighborhood with a typical parking problem. That's One Liberty Place in Center City "just a few" blocks straight ahead.

North Philadelphia

North Philadelphia, much of which looks just like this, is big, simply laid out, and often today getting the makeover it deserves. Back in the day, there were "country" estates up this way. Exactly where The Greater Northeast (as locals call it) begins is hard to say.

(above)

Under the Golden Dome

Buried in the Spring Garden neighborhood is the world's largest Ukrainian Catholic cathedral, the Cathedral of the Immaculate Conception of the Blessed Virgin Mary.

(left)

Murals Over Graffiti

Since 1984, Philadelphia's Mural Arts Program, largest in the nation, has created more than 2,300 murals celebrating the arts, nature, community, heroes and more. This elaborate 8-story one on North Broad Street, called *Common Threads*, is the city's tallest.

Whose Shoes

Lehigh Avenue is witness to a strange urban schoolboy custom, which just may have its roots (and certainly its laces) in Philadelphia. It probably has as much to do with boasting as with bullying, not to mention boosting sneaker sales for Nike et al.

Pat's King of Steaks

"Thousands a day" is how many of Philly's trademark sandwiches Pat's ("oldest in the world, undisputed") sells on 9th Street. Geno's next door might argue with the "King of," as would Jim's on South Street, and a thousand others. But the consensus is that the steak sandwich rules here, especially in South Philadelphia.

(right and below)

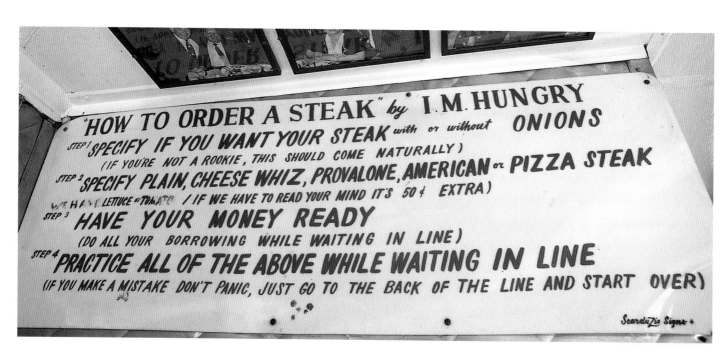

"HOW TO ORDER A STEAK" by I.M. HUNGRY

STEP 1 SPECIFY IF YOU WANT YOUR STEAK with or without ONIONS
(IF YOU'RE NOT A ROOKIE, THIS SHOULD COME NATURALLY)

STEP 2 SPECIFY PLAIN, CHEESE WHIZ, PROVALONE, AMERICAN or PIZZA STEAK
WE HAVE LETTUCE or TOMATO / IF WE HAVE TO READ YOUR MIND IT'S 50¢ EXTRA)

STEP 3 HAVE YOUR MONEY READY
(DO ALL YOUR BORROWING WHILE WAITING IN LINE)

STEP 4 PRACTICE ALL OF THE ABOVE WHILE WAITING IN LINE
(IF YOU MAKE A MISTAKE DON'T PANIC, JUST GO TO THE BACK OF THE LINE AND START OVER)

Scarduzio Signs

(above and left)

Life in the Italian Market

You loved two-term Philadelphia Mayor Frank Rizzo—or you didn't—but he was a hero in South Philly. And that's especially true around the Italian Market, largest and oldest (125 years) working outdoor market nationwide, where he's murally immortalized. Produce, fish, cheese, meats and game, you'll find it all here.

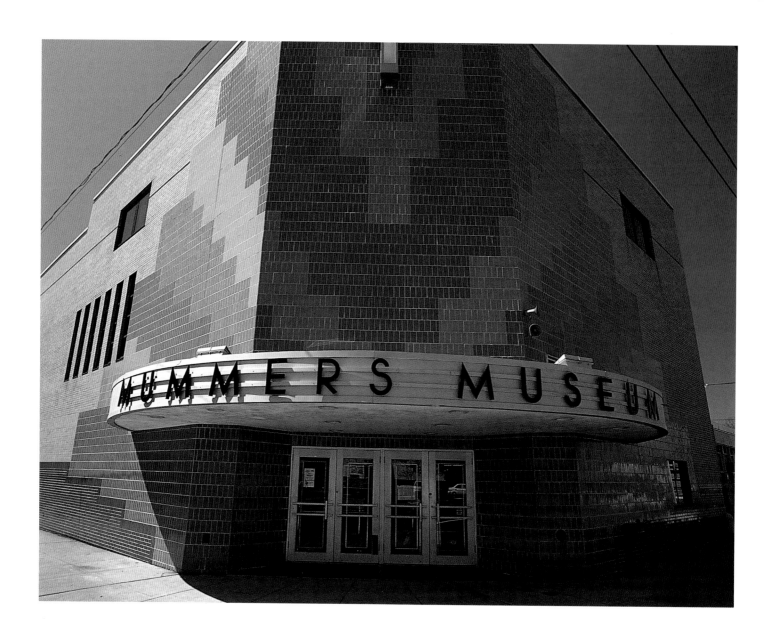

(above and left)

"Oh, Dem Golden Slippers"

You'll hear that and a great many other songs as the Mummers parade up Broad Street on New Year's Day. To say this Mardi Gras in Philly is tradition is to understate. It's passion! City Council blessed the annual gambol to City Hall back in 1901. If you miss the parade, get the idea at the (New Year's Shooters and) Mummers Museum, Two Street (as it's called) and Washington Avenue.

Mummers

Mummers (German for *mask*) vie for cash prizes each New Year's Day. Some 30,000 of them, members of String Bands, Fancies, Comics and Fancy Brigades, practice feverishly all year long to strut their stuff on this day of days.

(above)

Boathouse (Reflection) Row

Looking from the fish ladder on West River Drive, this rowing mecca's boathouses appear to double up across the Schuylkill River.

(opposite)

The Heart of Logan Circle

The Swann Memorial Fountain (or The Fountain of Three Rivers) is architect Wilson Eyre, Jr.'s tribute to Dr. Wilson Cary Swann who founded the Philadelphia Fountain Society. Sculptor Alexander Stirling Calder's male Indian figure represents the Delaware River.

(above, left and opposite)

Nights for Lights

Admittedly, there aren't fireworks every night in Philadelphia. It just seems that way. Long gone are the days when you had to wait for the Fourth. Now they happen regularly, whether outside the Art Museum, on the waterfront, or in the ballpark. And through all seasons, Philadelphia's a well-lit city at night, from outlined Boathouse Row, to illuminated Ben Franklin Bridge, to the message-bearing PECO Energy building.

Good Night, Philly

Philadelphia never really sleeps at night, and it never takes the day off from sharing its history, culture, recreation and distinct character again with each sunrise. Day and night, William Penn atop City Hall still presides over the very special place to which he so humbly gave birth.